A Glut
of
Plums

Ann Carr

Illustrated by
Martin MacKeown

MEREHURST PRESS
LONDON

*The Publishers wish to thank
Rosemary Wilkinson and Malcolm Saunders
for their help with this book.*

First published 1988 by Merehurst Press
5 Great James Street
London WC1N 3DA

Produced by
Malcolm Saunders Publishing Ltd
26 Ornan Road, London NW3 4QB

ISBN 1 85391 000 7

Photoset in Linotype Ehrhardt
by Fakenham Photosetting Limited
Printed in Spain

CONTENTS

FOREWORD

In good years the plum tree produces a bumper crop and its branches are so heavy with fruit there is a real fear that they may snap off and spoil the tree. In such years prices of the fruit come tumbling down daily and shops and market stalls are almost giving away the abundant fruit. And now with a variety of imported plums, the fruit is available all year round, which makes us less than ever able to cope with the gluts of our own garden or market crops. But we really should consume our own home produce first, if we don't want the delicious plums to vanish from the markets and to rot on the ground.

The versatile recipes in this book for both savoury and sweet dishes will enable you to use your glut for immediate meals or as delicious preserves for the store cupboard.

INTRODUCTION

The plum is a hybrid between the sloe, a beautiful and tiny deep purple, blue-bloomed plum with a bitter taste when you bite into its green flesh, and the red and yellow cherry-plum, small, sweet and scented. The wild cherry-plum is now rare and most people keep secret any trees they know of, guarding the crops for their own family's gathering.

Plums seem to have originated in western Asia where the two species, sloe and wild cherry-plum, hybridized naturally. Damsons take their name from Damascus in Syria, where the first early cultivation started. Probably other small, dark, strong-flavoured plums also originated in this area, though only the damson has kept its beautiful name.

Plums have been cultivated since classical times and a true breed, such as the damson, will still taste much the same as it did then.

There are many varieties of plums in many sizes, some almost as small as cherries; many shapes, ovoid to round, and many shades of blues, purples, reds, greens and yellows – some plums are almost black. There are delicious honey-sweet plums; plums that when ripe are still acid; cooking plums, tart and sharp and excellent to use and plums with pink flesh, green flesh and yellow flesh. The greengage – so delicious a dessert fruit – is in fact a plum, so called, it is said, after Sir William Gage, who first brought the trees to England from France in 1724. And we must remember that the poor, despised, dried prune once hung beautiful and succulent on a tree in a plum orchard.

There are something like a thousand varieties of plum in Europe. Unfortunately

fewer and fewer varieties are being produced commercially. In California, where the bulk of America's plums are grown, there are some forty varieties still produced commercially but only ten or twelve of them are grown in any great quantity.

Plums are the most widely distributed of the stone fruits. Plum orchards are planted all through Europe – from Italy in the south

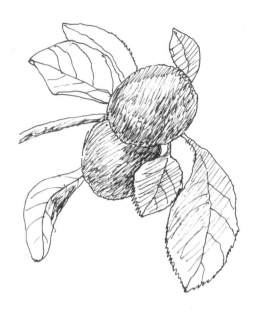

to Scandinavia in the north. Yugoslavia is the largest European producer of plums, where the countryside is made beautiful by the plum blossom. One can stop almost anywhere on a quiet country road and picnic beneath a plum tree. Very probably the owner will come and encourage you to pick his plums for your dessert: delicious, sweet, black plums, eaten warm in the sun. Yugoslavia also produces Sljivoviça – the fiery liqueur made from plums. This is the most

14

widely known but France, Germany and Switzerland all produce their own excellent plum liqueurs.

Germany is the next biggest plum producer in Europe with a tree potential that in some years can equal that of America. Much of America's crop of plums is made into prunes dried in dehydrators or the sun.

Plum trees, to crop reliably, need a hot summer, cold winter and warm spring but will grow in any warm, temperate climate. Apart from good soil management, which they do respond to, plum trees are relatively easy to grow as, once they come into fruit bearing, they do not require much pruning. This makes them a good tree for the home fruit gardener.

COOKS' NOTES

1. Unless specific details are given in the individual recipes, the following apply:
– spoon measurements are level
– sugar is granulated
– eggs are standard size
2. Follow either the imperial measurements or the metric but do not mix them, as they have been calculated separately.
3. As individual oven temperatures vary, use the timings in the recipes as a guide. Always preheat your oven or grill.

The Recipes

STARTERS

Plums for starters instead of puddings – who ever heard of such an idea? But plums make very good starters indeed. They go well with ham, are helped by a subtle marinade, make shells for stuffings, can be successfully used instead of melon or fresh figs and, when there is an abundance of them, will make an equally good and much cheaper accompaniment to that expensive luxury: Parma ham.

A Fruit Soup of Plums

Fruit soups are common in Germany and are refreshing and delicious starters.

Serves 3–4

1 lb (500 g) ripe plums, stoned

2 oz (60 g) ground almonds

1 teaspoon ground cinnamon

a very little salt and freshly ground white pepper

10 fl oz (315 ml) cold clear stock, meat or vegetable – stock cubes will do

1 spring onion, finely chopped

2 tablespoons dry white wine

Place plums in a blender or food processor and purée. Stir in almonds, cinnamon, salt and pepper, mixing well. Add stock and spring onion, mix again and leave to infuse in the fridge for 4 to 6 hours. Stir in wine just before serving.

Plums with Parma Ham

A simple, quick starter. The expense of the Parma ham is offset by accompanying it with your glut-plums rather than with figs which are also expensive.

Any sweet dessert plum will do. Peel, halve and stone the plums and arrange on a dish with the thinnest possible slices of Parma ham. It is important to skin the plums for their tough skins would spoil the dish.

To skin plums: really ripe plums should be easy to skin. If skins are difficult, make a small slit in the skin and soak for a minute or two in boiling water as you would tomatoes.

The Violet and Premorden Plum-trees are very great bearing trees.

(1657, Austin, Fruit Trees)

Rollmops with Plums, Mustard & Tarragon Sauce

Serves 4
about 12 oz (375 g) ripe plums
4 rollmops
sprigs of tarragon, to garnish
2 teaspoons French mustard
1 tablespoon chopped fresh tarragon
2 teaspoons soft brown sugar
6 fl oz (185 ml) thick sour cream

Halve and stone three or four of the plums
and arrange on a serving dish with rollmops.
Decorate with tarragon sprigs. Halve, stone
and roughly chop remaining plums. Place in
a bowl and add mustard, chopped tarragon,
sugar and cream. Gently mix together, pour
into a pretty bowl and serve with the rollmops.

21

Plum & Avocado Salad

Choose ripe avocados and plums. For four people you will need two avocados and eight plums.

Peel, halve and stone the plums. Toss in a vinaigrette dressing (made with two-thirds olive oil to one-third wine vinegar) and leave to marinate for half an hour.

To assemble, halve and stone avocado. Fill centre with half a plum. Fill plum centre with a teaspoonful of the following mixture:

chopped fresh parsley
chopped fresh chives
chopped almonds
salt and freshly ground black pepper

Arrange on plates with the remaining marinated plums. Serve accompanied by a vinaigrette to which you have added some of the chopped parsley and chives.

Little Jack Horner, we fear, misapplies the word plum, when he calls a dried raisin, or currant, by that name. The bullace pudding, the prune pudding, and the damascene pudding, are better entitled to be called plum-puddings than the currant, or raisin, puddings which have usurped that appellation.

(1813, W. Taylor)

Plum & Herb Vinaigrette

A refreshing starter and good for slimmers. Also nice with cold meats or to accompany bread and cheese.

Serves 4–5

1 1/2 lb (750 g) plums, the riper the better

2 teaspoons chopped fresh tarragon

1 teaspoon chopped fresh mint

1 small head crisp lettuce or 1/2 large crisp lettuce, to serve

VINAIGRETTE

3 fl oz (90 ml) olive oil

2 tablespoons wine vinegar

1/2 teaspoon Dijon mustard

salt and freshly ground black pepper, to taste

Wash and dry plums, halve and remove stones. Put into a bowl and sprinkle with herbs. Put all the vinaigrette ingredients into a screw-topped jar and shake well to mix. Pour over plums. Toss thoroughly but gently and leave to absorb the flavours for 30 minutes. To serve, shred crispy lettuce finely and arrange on a shallow serving dish, spoon over the plums and their juices.

Plum culture is a lottery: for plums either fruit too lightly or they break the tree and glut the market.
(1902, Daily Chronicle)

Marinated Plums

This is quite a filling starter and would make a light luncheon or supper dish. Smoked haddock goes well with fruits. It is best to use smoked haddock that is uncoloured and has not been painted with a commercial dye.

4 plums per person
juice of 1½ lemons
1 tablespoon brandy
1 clove garlic
2 oz (60 g) smoked haddock per person
juice of 2 oranges
freshly ground black pepper
plums or sprigs of parsley or small lettuce leaves, to garnish

Skin, halve and stone plums. Mix together juice of 1 lemon, brandy and half the clove of garlic, chopped. Pour over plums and leave to marinate for 6 hours.

Skin smoked haddock and cut into strips. Place in a shallow dish. Mix together remaining lemon juice, orange juice, pepper and remaining half of garlic, crushed. Pour over haddock strips and leave for 6 hours.

To serve, arrange strips of haddock and marinated plums on individual plates. Garnish with half a plum, unskinned or sprigs of parsley or small lettuce leaves. Thin slices of brown bread and butter are good with this starter.

Note: The haddock may be prepared and left, covered, overnight in the fridge to marinate. Do not leave plums longer than 6 hours, they tend to discolour.

Stuffed Plums

These are perhaps not strictly speaking a starter but an appetizer or a snack to serve with drinks in the garden. A German, or German-type, wine would accompany these stuffed plum halves especially well.

For this dish it is not necessary to peel the plums: just halve and fill with any of the suggested stuffings. Curd cheese forms the basic ingredient in all the stuffings. The other ingredients add flavouring and texture. I have based the recipes on using approximately 2 oz (60 g) curd cheese. In each case, place ingredients in a bowl and mix well. You can adjust cheese and flavourings as you like,

26

according to taste and to what drinks the stuffed plums are to accompany.

1

curd cheese (sieved if not smooth)
finely chopped celery
1/2 teaspoon minced onion
1/2 teaspoon grated orange peel
salt and pepper

2

cream cheese (curd will do)
a few currants
finely chopped fresh parsley
1/2 teaspoon minced onion
1/4 teaspoon curry paste

3

curd cheese (sieved if not smooth)
a little smoked fish, e.g. haddock, smoked
salmon bits or smoked trout
1/2 teaspoon grated lemon peel
salt and pepper

4

curd cheese (sieved if not smooth)
chopped ham
a little mayonnaise
1/4 teaspoon mustard
pepper

Greengages

Stuffed Greengages

Greengages are the most delicious and delicately flavoured of all the plum family, perhaps this is why there seem to be so few recipes for their use in cooking. However, I think that this stuffing doesn't detract too much from their subtlety.

Greengages will discolour when cut, so work fast and mix the stuffing first. It can be prepared in advance and the fruit cut and filled just before serving.

For each person you will need:
1 tablespoon cream cheese
1/4 teaspoon curry paste or powder
1/2 teaspoon icing sugar
salt and pepper, to taste
1/2 teaspoon very finely chopped cucumber using the skin and flesh nearest the skin
3 ripe greengages
a few thin slices of cucumber, to garnish

In a bowl mix together cream cheese, curry paste or powder, sugar, salt and pepper, then fold in chopped cucumber. Wash fruit, cut in half lengthwise and remove stones. Fill the hollows with cream cheese mixture and garnish with cucumber slices cut into quarters.

MAIN COURSE DISHES

We are very conventional when we think of sweet and savoury. Sweet and sour – we immediately think of the Chinese pork dish. Meat and fruit? Well, yes: duck with orange or black cherries; turkey with cranberries and tongue with raisin sauce. But beef – that king of meats – must be accompanied only by Yorkshire pudding and horseradish sauce with a good gravy for the vegetables. Yet we do use sweet and sour: we are great chutney, sauce and relish eaters, though mostly only with cold meats. The fruits of those over-burdened plum trees could well be used up in place of the chutney, currants, oranges, cherries and cranberries. Try plums with duck instead of cherries, they are excellent. Other delicious recipes for simple hot main course dishes are given in this chapter to help use up that surplus of plums.

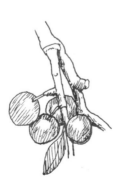

Its fruit is called Wilde Pruime from its plum-like eating flesh.

(1886, Treas. Bot.)

A White Fish Dish with Plums

This might seem strange to cook but do try it for it really is very delicious.

6–8 oz (185–250 g) white fish per person – sole, plaice or halibut are good

2–3 oz (60–90 g) butter

1 1/2 plums per person, skinned, halved and stoned

2 tablespoons white wine

salt and freshly ground white pepper

chopped fresh parsley, to garnish

Ask your fishmonger to fillet and skin the fish for you.

Gently melt about 2 oz (60 g) of the butter in a large frying pan. Add fish and cook very slowly. Fresh fish needs very gentle – and very little – cooking. In a separate pan cook plums in a little butter for approximately 5 minutes. Add wine and heat thoroughly, then add salt and pepper. To serve, place fish on serving platter, pour over sauce, decorate with plums and sprinkle with parsley.

Chicken with Plums & Almonds

I like to make this dish with the first of the late plum crop but it could be made with pre-soaked prunes in the winter.

Serves 4
4 chicken breasts
1 egg, lightly beaten
2 oz (60 g) blanched almonds, finely chopped
2 oz (60 g) butter
salt and pepper, to taste
8 plums, halved and stoned
1/4–1/2 teaspoon cinnamon

Dry chicken breasts on absorbent kitchen paper and dip them first in the egg, then in the almonds. In a frying pan melt 1 oz (30 g) of the butter and gently fry chicken breasts for 4 to 5 minutes on each side depending on their size, until they are cooked through. Add salt and pepper, transfer to a warm serving plate and keep warm. Melt remaining butter and gently fry plums for 1 to 2 minutes on each side. Sprinkle cut sides with cinnamon, arrange round chicken pieces and serve.

Plum & Pork Casserole

Serves 4–5

1 tablespoon oil

2 large onions, finely chopped

2 rashers smoked bacon, roughly chopped

2 lb (1 kg) chopped lean pork or 4 pork chops

1 lb (500 g) plums

2 cloves or ¼ teaspoon ground cloves

20 fl oz (625 ml) cider

salt and pepper, to taste

Place oil in a flameproof casserole, add onions and bacon and fry gently for 5 minutes. Add the other ingredients and cook gently on top of the stove or in the oven, at 160 °C (325 °F/Gas 3), for about an hour, until pork is tender but not dry.

Plums with Gammon & Fried Bread

A tasty lunch or supper dish, made in a matter of moments.

Serves 6

6 gammon rashers, medium cut, rinds reserved

6 plums, stoned

3 sage leaves

2 teaspoons oil

salt and pepper, to taste

crispy fried bread, to serve

Lay rashers out flat and place a plum on each rasher. Place half a sage leaf on top of each plum, then roll up tightly and secure with a wooden toothpick or cocktail stick. Place in a frying pan with oil, add salt and pepper and fry gently for about 12 minutes, turning once, until gammon is cooked. Serve on slices of crispy fried bread.

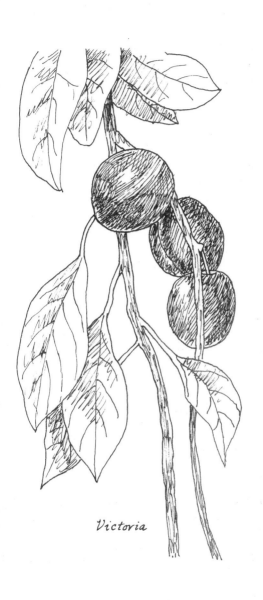

Victoria

Plums with Beef & Sesame Seeds

For this recipe you need only the cheapest cuts of beef. As with all meat and fruit stews, the fruit seems to help tenderize what might otherwise be a tough cut as well as quite definitely improving the flavour.

Serves 4–5

2 tablespoons olive oil or other oil or cooking fat

2 lb (1 kg) stewing beef, cubed

1/4 teaspoon ground ginger

1 teaspoon cinnamon

1 lb (500 g) plums

10 pickling onions or other small onions, peeled

10 fl oz (315 ml) water

salt and pepper

1 teaspoon rose water, if desired

1–2 tablespoons toasted sesame seeds

Heat oil or fat in a heavy-bottomed pan, add meat and spices and cook gently for 5 to 6 minutes, turning occasionally to ensure meat is well coated with oil and spices. Halve and stone 8 oz (250 g) of the plums and add to pan with onions and water. Bring to the boil, cover with a tight-fitting lid, lower heat and simmer very gently for about 2 hours, until meat is tender. Fifteen minutes before end of cooking time, add remainder of plums, halved and stoned, together with salt and pepper. When plums are cooked, test again for seasoning and adjust if necessary. Add rose water, if desired, pour into serving dish and sprinkle with 1 or 2 tablespoons toasted sesame seeds.

Plum & Pigeon Tagine

This is not a classic tagine (Middle-eastern meat and fruit stew) but an adaptation of my own for using up two gluts in the same dish. Often in the country we get given a huge sackful of pigeons after the farmers have had a Saturday afternoon's shoot when the wheat has just been sown. This recipe is quick to prepare and delicious.

Serves 4

4 plump pigeons

1 large onion

2 thick slices bread, brown or white, crusts removed

1 lb (500 g) plums

livers from the pigeons or 2 oz (60 g) chicken livers, chopped

1 oz (30 g) butter, melted

salt and pepper

1 oz (30 g) blanched, chopped almonds

1 egg yolk

1 tablespoon oil or cooking fat

10 fl oz (315 ml) red wine

Wash insides of pigeons and dry thoroughly. Peel onion and halve. Chop one half finely and reserve for stuffing, roughly chop the other half to cook with pigeons.

To make the stuffing, place bread in a blender or food processor and process to crumbs. Halve, stone and chop 4 of the plums, place in a bowl and stir in breadcrumbs, livers and melted butter. Add salt, pepper, almonds and egg yolk and mix well together. Fill pigeons with this mixture.

Place oil or fat in a heavy casserole. Add chopped onion and pack pigeons in carefully. Pour over wine and cover tightly. Cook in a cool oven, 150 °C (300 °F/Gas 2), for 1½–2 hours. Meanwhile halve and stone remaining plums and add to casserole 45 minutes before end of cooking time.

(New England) beach-plum jelly brings handsome prices, but it is almost always scarce because the recalcitrant bushes have baffled all efforts to grow them commercially. Cultivation seems to offend them. When planted in rich, well-fertilized soil, they grow tall but produce hardly any fruit. Even when planted in the poor sandy soil that they seem to prefer, they sulk in captivity. Apparently they need the stress and adversity that is inseparable from life along the shore.

(Jonathan Norton Leonard)

Plums with Rabbit & Mustard Seeds

This is a variation of the classic French dish of rabbit with mustard sauce. Check regularly when cooking, as rabbit, like chicken, can be rather a dry meat if overcooked.

Serves 4
1 oz (30 g) butter
1 small onion, finely chopped
2 lb (1 kg) chopped rabbit or rabbit pieces
8 oz (250 g) plums, halved and stoned
2 tablespoons brandy
10 fl oz (315 ml) double (heavy) cream
salt and pepper
1 tablespoon mustard seeds, toasted
chopped fresh parsley, to serve

Melt butter in a heavy saucepan with a tight-fitting lid, add onion and fry gently for a few minutes, do not brown. Add rabbit, plums and brandy and cook very gently for 5 minutes, stirring constantly, then cover tightly and simmer for 20 minutes, taking care not to burn. Stir in cream, cover and cook for a further 30 to 45 minutes, then add salt, pepper and mustard seeds. Serve hot sprinkled with chopped parsley.

Baked Plums with Onions

Serves 4
1 lb (500 g) pickling onions
2 tablespoons olive oil
2 cloves garlic, chopped
1 lb (500 g) plums
1 teaspoon coriander seeds, whole
juice of 2 oranges
salt and pepper, to taste

To peel onions, blanch for 5 minutes in boiling water, strain and plunge into a basin full of cold water. Peel at once. Heat oil in a heavy flameproof casserole with a tight-fitting lid, add garlic and onions and fry gently for 5 to 7 minutes, stirring occasionally. Add plums, coriander, orange juice, salt and pepper. Cover tightly and bake in a moderate oven, 180 °C (350 °F/Gas 4), for 30 minutes. This dish can also be cooked gently on top of the stove. Serve on its own as a light luncheon dish or as an accompaniment to game or roast meats.

The black Damascen, the Morocco, the Barbary,
the Myrobalan, the Apricock Plumb, a delicate
Plumb that parts clean from the Stone.

(1707, Mortimer)

Pork Fillet with Damson Stuffing

This recipe feeds six to eight. It could be made with prunes, in which case omit the sugar.

2 pork fillets (tenderloin), cut open for
stuffing
2 oz (60 g) butter
2 onions, chopped
8 oz (250 g) damsons, stoned if possible
1 tablespoon demerara (brown) sugar
6 rashers smoked bacon
1/2 teaspoon caraway seeds, if desired
1/2 large, hard, white cabbage, finely
shredded
6 fl oz (185 ml) cider
salt and pepper, to taste

Spread fillets out flat. Melt butter in a frying pan, add onion and cook gently until tender, but do not brown. Spread half the onions over fillets, then add a row of damsons. Sprinkle with sugar, lay a bacon rasher on top of each fillet, roll up tightly and tie with string. Chop remaining four bacon rashers and mix with remaining onions, caraway seeds and cabbage. Place half this mixture in the bottom of a heavy casserole with a tight-fitting lid, put in fillets and cover with the remaining cabbage mixture. Pour over cider, add salt and pepper, cover tightly and bake in a moderate oven, 180 °C (350 °F/Gas 4), for 1 hour or until fillets are cooked.

Damsons

Baked Pork Chops with Damsons & Honey

This is best made with fresh damsons but could be made with the bottled fruit or with Pickled Damsons (see page 77) – in which case leave out the spice and add 1 tablespoon extra honey.

Serves 4
1 tablespoon cooking oil
4 lean pork chops
8 oz (250 g) damsons
1/4 teaspoon ground allspice
2 tablespoons clear honey
4 fl oz (125 ml) white wine
salt and pepper, to taste

In a flameproof casserole with a tight-fitting lid heat oil and quickly brown chops on both sides. Mix together all the other ingredients, pour over chops, cover and bake in a moderate oven, 190 °C (375 °F/Gas 5), for 45 minutes or until tender. Skim off as many stones as possible before serving.

A cherry year's a merry year,
A sloe year's a woe year,
A haw year's a braw year,
An apple year's a drappin' year,
A plum year's a glum year.
(1664, Poor Robin Almanac)

PLUMS FOR PUDDINGS

This seems the obvious use for plums, yet the variety of ways in which they are served is often limited to stewed plums with custard or ice cream and plum tart, which doesn't do justice to this versatile fruit. Plums have a marvellous facility for blending with other things, such as nuts, wines, liqueurs and spices. They can be stored as delicate purées or frozen into delicious sorbets and ice creams.

Plum Soufflé

Serves 4–6

1 lb (500 g) plums

2 tablespoons water

2 oz (60 g) butter

1 tablespoon plain flour ⎫
1 tablespoon cornflour ⎬ *sifted together*

6 oz (185 g) ground almonds

6 fl oz (185 ml) white wine, or cider, or apple juice

4 oz (125 g) sugar

3 eggs, separated

2 tablespoons crushed biscuit crumbs

icing sugar, for dusting

In a saucepan with a tight-fitting lid, gently stew plums in water for about 10 minutes.

Cool slightly, remove stones, then purée plums and juice in a blender or food processor. Melt butter carefully in a saucepan – do not brown. Remove from the heat and stir in sifted flours and ground almonds, mixing well together. Pour on wine, cider or apple juice, mix well, then add purée, return to the heat and allow to cook gently, stirring constantly until the mixture thickens. Cool slightly, stir in sugar, then add egg yolks one by one, beating well in between. Whisk egg whites until stiff, then fold into plum mixture. Butter a soufflé dish liberally, dust well with biscuit crumbs, making sure sides and bottom are well coated and pour in soufflé mixture. Bake in a hot oven, 200 °C (400 °F/ Gas 6), for 40 to 50 minutes. Dust with icing sugar and serve at once.

a good, handsome, plum-cheekt wench or lasse.
(1598, Florio)

Plum Jalousie

A jalousie is a fruit tart covered on top with a layer of pastry in which slits have been cut to make a lattice or shutter effect. I make mine like a 'turnover' and snip down the top with kitchen scissors.

Serves 6

8 oz (250 g) puff pastry or Rough Puff Pastry (see page 85)

2 tablespoons cake crumbs

1 lb (500 g) plums, cut in half lengthwise and stoned

4 oz (125 g) sugar

Roll out pastry into a square – it should not be more than ¼ in (0.5 cm) thick. Place it on a greased baking sheet. Dust half pastry square with cake crumbs, leaving ¼ in (0.5 cm) clear at sides. Lay plums on top, cut side uppermost, and sprinkle with sugar. Dampen pastry edges with cold water, fold over and press well together. With kitchen scissors or a sharp knife, slash down the length of the jalousie at 1½ in (4 cm) intervals. Bake in a hot oven, 200 °C (400 °F/Gas 6), for 25 minutes until pastry is well-risen, golden brown and crisp.

Hasty Plum Turnovers

Serves 6

12 oz (375 g) plums, halved lengthwise and stoned

4 oz (125 g) sugar

1 teaspoon cinnamon, or grated peel of 1 orange

1 lb (500 g) Rough Puff or Shortcrust Pastry (see pages 84 and 85)

milk, for glazing

Chop plums roughly into a bowl, mix sugar and spice or peel together and add to plums. Roll out pastry ¼ in (0.5 cm) thick and cut into squares 6 × 6 in (15 × 15 cm). Place a spoonful of plum mixture in middle of each pastry square, dampen edges with water, fold over into a triangle and press edges together. Place turnovers on a greased baking sheet, brush with milk and bake in a hot oven, 220 °C (425 °F/Gas 7), for 20 to 30 minutes until golden.

Plum tart ... Seasonable, with various kinds of plums, from the beginning of August to the beginning of October.

(Beeton's Everyday Cook Book)

Plum & Almond Tart

A recipe using puff pastry and ground almonds to absorb the juice. It is a classic Swiss recipe and the plums used should be small and tart.

Serves 6

8 oz (250 g) puff pastry or Rough Puff Pastry (see page 85)

1–1½ lb (500–750 g) plums, halved and stoned

4 oz (125 g) sugar

4 oz (125 g) ground almonds

double (heavy) cream, to serve

Roll out pastry to fit an 8 × 12 in (20 × 30 cm) Swiss roll tin. Grease tin and line with pastry. Lay plums on pastry as close together as possible and sprinkle on first sugar, then ground almonds. Bake in a hot oven, 200 °C (400 °F/Gas 6), for 20 to 30 minutes, until pastry is golden and plums cooked. Serve hot with cream.

Plum Charlotte with Almond Topping

A rich version of a classic pudding.

Serves 6–8
1½ lb (750 g) plums, halved and stoned
2 tablespoons dark rum
5 oz (155 g) demerara (brown) sugar
4 oz (125 g) butter
4–5 slices white bread
3 egg yolks
2 oz (60 g) plain flour
2 oz (60 g) ground almonds
cream, to serve

Place plums in a saucepan with tight-fitting lid, add rum, cover and simmer until just cooked – about 10 minutes. Remove from the heat, add 3 oz (90 g) of the sugar, stir

gently, cover and leave aside. Butter slices of bread generously and butter the sides and bottom of a 7 in (17.5 cm) soufflé dish thickly. Line the bottom and sides with some slices of bread. Beat egg yolks well and fold into plum mixture. Place a layer of plums in the lined dish, cover with buttered bread, add another layer of plums and so on, finishing with a layer of plums. Set aside.

Place flour and ground almonds in a bowl and add remaining butter, cut up into small pieces – you should have about 2 oz (60 g). Rub butter in with the fingertips until the mixture looks like fine breadcrumbs (or process in a food processor), add remaining sugar and mix well. Sprinkle this mixture on top of the final layer of plums. Bake in a moderate oven, 190 °C (375 °F/Gas 5), for 40 to 50 minutes. Serve hot with cream.

Plum Upside-Down Cake

Serves 6

4½ oz (140 g) butter

4½ oz (140 g) sugar

*8 oz (250 g) plums, halved lengthwise
and stoned*

2 eggs

4 oz (125 g) self-raising flour

Melt ½ oz (15 g) of the butter in a saucepan, add ½ oz (15 g) of the sugar, then mix in plums, stirring until well coated. Pour into an 8 in (20 cm) sponge cake tin, coating the sides with the juice. Leave to one side while making the cake mixture. Cream remaining butter and sugar together in a bowl until light and fluffy, then beat in eggs, one by one, and fold in flour. Spoon over plums, spreading evenly. Bake in a moderate oven, 190 °C (375 °F/Gas 5), for 15 to 20 minutes until sponge is pale golden and the middle is firm to touch. Turn onto a serving plate. Serve hot.

Little Jack Horner
Sat in the corner,
Eating a Christmas pie;
He put in his thumb,
And pulled out a plum,
And said 'What a good boy am I'.

Plum Pancakes

Make pancakes following the basic recipe on page 86 and fill with the following recipe. This mixture will keep in the fridge for up to 48 hours.

Serves 6–8
1 lb (500 g) plums, halved and stoned
2 oz (60 g) butter
3 oz (90 g) sugar
1 tablespoon brandy
2 oz (60 g) ground almonds

In a saucepan with a tight-fitting lid sweat plums in butter and sugar for 7 to 10 minutes until tender, then stir in brandy and ground almonds. Fill the hot pancakes and serve at once.

The song of men divinely wise
Who look and see in starry skies
Not stars so much as robins' eyes,
And when these pale away
Hear flocks of shiney pleidades
Among the plums and apple trees
Sing in the summer day.

(1871, Ralph Hodgson)

Plum Queen of Puddings

Queen of Puddings is a traditional English dish made with raspberry jam. This version uses plums.

Serves 4–6
20 fl oz (625 ml) milk
1½ oz (45 g) butter
4 oz (125 g) breadcrumbs
grated peel of 1 orange
5 egg yolks
2 oz (60 g) sugar
8 oz (250 g) plums, halved and stoned
2 tablespoons plum jam
1 tablespoon chopped blanched almonds
3 egg whites
4 oz (125 g) caster sugar

Heat milk and butter in a saucepan, but do not allow to boil. Pour over breadcrumbs, add orange peel and leave to soak while you mix together egg yolks and sugar, then add these to the milk mixture. Butter a 3 pint (2 litre) pie dish. Lay plums on the bottom, pour over egg and milk mixture, then place dish in a tin of hot water and bake in a moderate oven, 180°C (350°F/Gas 4), for 30 to 40 minutes until set. Remove from the oven, spread with jam and sprinkle with almonds.

In a bowl beat egg whites until stiff, add half the caster sugar, beat again, then fold in the remaining sugar. Spread roughly over jam and bake in a cool oven, 150°C (300°F/ Gas 2), for 20 to 25 minutes until meringue begins to colour.

Fried Plums with Cinnamon Toast

Children love this as a tea-time treat; accompany it with a bowl of thick plain yogurt dusted with brown sugar.

For every slice of bread, brown or white, you will need 2 or 3 plums, depending on size, butter, ¼ teaspoon cinnamon and 1 teaspoon demerara or soft brown sugar.

In a frying pan gently melt 1 oz (30 g) butter, add the plums – halved and stoned – and fry for 4 to 5 minutes until tender; leave aside. Toast the bread, butter while hot, sprinkle with sugar and cinnamon, pile on the plums and serve at once.

Plum Sorbet

Serves 6–8

1 lb (500 g) plums, stones removed
4 fl oz (125 ml) white wine
8 fl oz (250 ml) water
6 oz (185 g) sugar
a strip of orange peel
2 egg whites

Poach plums in wine for 7 to 10 minutes. Sieve or purée in a blender or food processor and leave aside.

To make a sugar syrup, place water, sugar and orange peel together in a heavy saucepan and boil for 7 to 10 minutes, then leave to cool. When cool, mix sieved or puréed plums with syrup and freeze until nearly firm. Beat egg whites until stiff. Remove plum mixture from freezer and beat well, then fold in egg whites. Continue freezing until firm.

Damson Sorbet

A damson sorbet is delicious and can be made as for 'Plum Sorbet', but add lemon peel instead of orange peel and 1 teaspoon cinnamon to the damson purée.

Damson Ice Cream

Serves 6–8

4 egg yolks

4 oz (125 g) caster sugar

*10 fl oz (315 ml) thick damson purée (see
'Damson Tapioca', page 61, making half
quantity)*

*10 fl oz (315 ml) whipping cream and
10 fl oz (315 ml) double (heavy) cream or
20 fl oz (625 ml) double (heavy) cream*

In a bowl over a saucepan of simmering water beat egg yolks and sugar until thick and fluffy. Remove from the heat and leave to cool. When cold, stir in damson purée, then pour into a plastic container and freeze until mixture begins to set round the edges – 40 to 50 minutes. Whip creams together until stiff. Remove purée from freezer, mix well, then fold in cream. Freeze again until ice cream is firm.

Damson Tapioca

This is a damson purée set with the tapioca; it is both delicious and nourishing.

Serves 4–5
1 lb (500 g) damsons
20 fl oz (625 ml) water
1½ oz (45 g) pearl tapioca
6–8 oz (185–250 g) sugar

TO SERVE
sponge fingers or crisp biscuits
a bowl of yogurt and double (heavy) cream, mixed half and half

To make damson purée boil damsons in water in a saucepan until they are soft and mushy, 10 to 15 minutes. Press through a coarse sieve, or remove all stones and purée in a blender or food processor. Return purée to pan, add tapioca and cook together over a gentle heat until tapioca is soft and clear. When cooking is finished, remove from the heat and add sugar. Cool and pour into a glass serving dish. Serve with sponge fingers or crisp biscuits and a bowl of yogurt and cream.

As pees-coddes and pere-Ionettes, plomes and chiries.

(1393, Langland)

Damson Fool

Serves 6
6 fl oz (185 ml) double (heavy) cream
6 oz (185 g) caster sugar
6 fl oz (185 ml) plain yogurt
20 fl oz (625 ml) thick damson purée (see
'Damson Tapioca', page 61)

Whip cream with sugar in a bowl until stiff.
Fold in first yogurt, then damson purée and
pour into a pretty dish. Chill before serving.

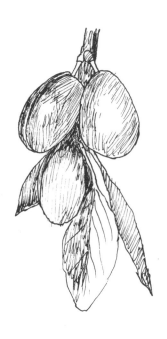

Greengages with Honey

A recipe for the 'not-so-ripe' gages.

Serves 4
1½ lb–2 lb (750 g–1 kg) greengages
6 fl oz (185 ml) white wine
2 tablespoons honey

In a saucepan with a tight-fitting lid gently cook greengages with wine, taking care not to let the fruit go mushy – 10 to 15 minutes, depending on ripeness of fruit. Remove from the heat and stir in honey. Cool and serve.

Greengage, Fruit & Nut Salad

Serves 4–6

4 oz (125 g) sugar

8 fl oz (250 ml) water

1 lb (500 g) ripe greengages, halved and stoned

2–3 ripe pears

a small bunch ripe grapes, halved, pips removed

2 tablespoons chopped walnuts

Make a sugar syrup with sugar and water as described in the recipe for 'Plum Sorbet' (see page 59). Drop greengages into hot syrup at once, then peel pears, chop and add to syrup with the grapes. Leave aside to cool before adding walnuts. This fruit salad is nicer if served unchilled; it will not keep for more than a few hours. Should you wish to keep it longer, toss fruits in 2 tablespoons lemon juice before adding to syrup.

PLUMS FOR THE STORE CUPBOARD

Plums are ideal for the store cupboard: they make excellent chutneys and pickles; they can be spiced or preserved in brandy or they can be turned into delicious jams and purées.

There is hard work in preserving for the winter but great satisfaction in knowing that your store cupboard will hold all sorts of good things that cannot be bought off the supermarket shelves. And cooking for the store cupboard is stimulating and creative, using herbs and spices to add piquancy to the fruit and producing a variety of preserves both for the home table and to give away as presents.

The higher the plum-tree,
The sweeter the plum.
The richer the cobbler,
The blacker his thumb.

Plum Purée

If you really have so many plums that you cannot pickle or jam them all, purée them, freeze and use later.

1 lb (500 g) plums
3 tablespoons water

Place plums and water in a pan with a tight-fitting lid, cover and simmer together until soft, 10 to 15 minutes. Remove stones, purée in a blender or food processor, then freeze.

To come now to plums, there is a world of them: some of sundrie colours, others blacke and some againe white.

(1601, Holland: Pliny)

Plum Sauce

This is a plum sauce with a difference, the classic is a Chinese recipe, usually served with duck.

1 oz (30 g) butter
1 lb (500 g) plums, halved and stoned
1 clove garlic
¼ teaspoon ground allspice
1 tablespoon sugar
1 teaspoon grated lemon peel
2 teaspoons wine vinegar
6 fl oz (185 ml) sour cream

Melt butter in a saucepan with a tight-fitting lid, add plums, garlic and allspice. Cover and cook gently for 10 to 12 minutes until fruit is soft and mushy, stirring occasionally to prevent burning. When fruit is cooked, remove garlic, then purée the fruit in a blender or food processor. Return to saucepan, add sugar, lemon peel and vinegar, heat gently, then stir in sour cream. Serve with pork, hot gammon or game.

Plum Chutney

Oranges are often added to plum jams, I think they are better in chutneys.

3 oranges
3 lb (1.5 kg) plums, halved and stoned
1 lb (500 g) brown sugar
10 fl oz (315 ml) cider
1 clove garlic
8 allspice ⎫ *tied together*
1 in (2.5 cm) piece ⎬ *in a muslin bag*
fresh root ginger ⎭
10 fl oz (315 ml) cider vinegar

Cut oranges in half, discard pips and mince flesh. Place fruit in a preserving pan, add sugar and cider and heat gently, stirring constantly until sugar is dissolved. Add the muslin bag of spices and cook for 45 minutes. Next add vinegar, cook for a further 30 to 45 minutes, then remove spice bag, pour into warm jars (see page 88), cover and store in a cool, dark place.

The rule is, jam tomorrow and jam yesterday –
but never jam today.

(1871, Lewis Carroll, Through the Looking-
Glass)

Plum & Walnut Jam

Plums and walnuts seem to have a natural
affinity. This is a lovely jam and very easy to
make. Best made with plums of robust
flavour.

3 lb (1.5 kg) plums
8 fl oz (250 ml) water
3 lb (1.5 kg) sugar
8 oz (250 g) walnuts, roughly chopped

Pick over fruit and remove stalks or leaves.
Halve lengthwise and remove stones; it is not
necessary to remove all stones – it is difficult
with unripe fruit and some not-so-ripe
plums will increase the acidity and improve
the 'set', so don't worry. Place plums and
water in a preserving pan or large, heavy-
based saucepan and gently heat. When water
begins to boil, stir fruit, then simmer gently
for 25 to 30 minutes, until fruit is soft. Remove pan from heat and add sugar, stir, return to low heat and continue to stir until
sugar is dissolved. Increase heat, add walnuts
and boil hard for 15 to 30 minutes until set is
reached (see page 88). Pot (see page 88),
label and store in a cool, dark place.

There the huge sirloin reeked; hard by Plum-
porridge stood, and Christmas pye.
(1808, Scott, Marmion)

Dumps

An old-fashioned recipe for using up the end
of autumn fruits, usually made with apples,
pears and plums, dumped into a saucepan,
boiled with water and sugar to make jam. I
think it is much nicer without the apples.

1½ lb (750 g) pears
1½ lb (750 g) plums, halved and stoned
1 teaspoon grated orange peel
juice of 2 oranges
3 lb (1.5 kg) sugar

Peel and core pears, chop roughly and place
in a preserving pan. Add plums, orange peel
and juice. Heat gently over a very slow heat,
stirring constantly, for 10 to 15 minutes and
when fruit is soft, remove from the heat and
stir in sugar. Return to heat and cook gently
until sugar is dissolved, increase heat and
boil hard until 'set' is reached (see page 88) –
20 to 30 minutes. Pour into heated jars (see
page 88), cover and store in a cool place.

Plum & Orange Jam

1 orange
4 fl oz (125 ml) port
2 lb (1 kg) plums, halved and stoned
2 lb (1 kg) sugar

Halve orange, remove pips, mince, place in a bowl with port and leave to marinate overnight. Next day, in a preserving pan, gently heat together orange mixture and plums, stirring constantly to prevent burning. When fruit is warmed through, add sugar and dissolve slowly over a gentle heat, then increase the heat and boil until 'set' is reached (see page 88) – 20 to 30 minutes. Pot (see page 88) in warm jars, cover and store.

Plum Butter

This is rather like a curd and makes a good pie filling. It can be made without puréeing the fruit.

2 lb (1 kg) plums, halved and stoned
4 oz (125 g) butter
2 tablespoons water
6 oz (185 g) caster sugar
4 egg yolks
2 tablespoons rose water

Place plums, butter and water in a saucepan with a tight-fitting lid, cover and cook over a gentle heat until fruit is soft – 10 to 15 minutes. Transfer to a blender or food processor, if desired, and purée. In a bowl beat together sugar, egg yolks and rose water, then add to warm plum mixture and cook in the top of a double boiler until mixture begins to thicken – 20 to 30 minutes. Serve as a pudding or pot (see page 88), cover and store in the fridge for later use as a pie filling. It will keep for 6–8 weeks.

Prunes . . . they have not had enough to lay round their plum-porridge at Christmas.

(1698, W. King)

Plum Hooch

A recipe for well-flavoured, ripe and undamaged plums: make one year and eat the next. Serve in small quantities with thin biscuits.

Layer plums alternately with caster sugar in a crock or large earthenware container with a close-fitting lid, then cover with dark rum. Replace lid and store in a cool place. You can go on adding to the crock during the plum season. As this is an extravagant recipe I suggest you use only a small crock or jar.

Plums in Rum with Almonds

A more modest version of 'Plum Hooch' and more time consuming!

4 oz (125 g) sugar
10 fl oz (315 ml) water
peel of 1 orange
1 lb (500 g) plums
2 oz (60 g) blanched almonds
6 fl oz (185 ml) rum

In a saucepan boil sugar, water and orange peel together for 7 minutes. Remove peel and add plums and almonds. Boil gently for 5 minutes, then add rum and boil again for 2 to 3 minutes. Remove fruit with a slotted spoon and pack into hot jars, pour on hot syrup. Cover at once with airtight lids. Store in a cool, dark place. Keep for 4 to 6 months before eating.

To Preserve Plums Dry

This method of keeping plums for winter eating I first discovered in an old volume of house and kitchen notes and ideas called *Inquire Within*, published in 1867. The recipe I give is one of Mrs Beeton's, unchanged.

To every lb (500 g) of sugar allow ¼ pint (155 ml) of water.

Gather the plums when they are full-grown and just turning colour; prick them, put them into a saucepan of cold water, and set them on the fire until the water is on the point of boiling. Then take them out, drain them and boil them gently in syrup made with the above proportion of sugar and water; and if the plums shrink and will not take the sugar, prick them as they lie in the pan; give them another boil, skim and set them by. The next day add some more sugar, boiled almost to candy, to the fruit and syrup; put all together into a wide-mouthed jar, and place them in a cool oven for 2 nights; then drain the plums from the syrup, sprinkle a little powdered sugar over, and dry them in a cool oven.

Time – 15 to 20 minutes to boil the plums in the syrup.

Medlers, plowmes, perys, chesteyns.

(1366, Chaucer)

Pickled Plums

10 fl oz (315 ml) wine or cider vinegar
1 lb (500 g) sugar
few sprigs of rosemary
peel of 2 oranges
2 lb (1 kg) plums

In a saucepan boil together vinegar, sugar, a sprig of rosemary and peel of 1 orange for 5 minutes. Pour into a bowl and leave overnight to infuse. Next day, pick over fruit and remove stalks and any damaged plums. Add to pan with vinegar syrup, bring to the boil and cook gently until fruit is tender but still whole – 20 to 30 minutes. Remove plums using a slotted spoon, pack into clean storage jars, to which you have added the rest of the rosemary and orange peel, and pour over syrup. Seal, label and store in a cool place. The plums will be ready in 6 weeks but are better if kept longer.

Pickled Damsons

This is very easy to prepare, the fruit does not have to be stoned.

9 fl oz (280 ml) wine, red or white
15 fl oz (470 ml) wine vinegar, red or white
1 stick cinnamon
6 cloves stuck into an orange
3 lb (1.5 kg) damsons
1 lb (500 g) sugar

Pour wine and vinegar into a saucepan, add cinnamon and orange stuck with cloves and simmer over a very low heat for 30 minutes until spices have flavoured the liquor. Meanwhile place damsons in a large bowl. Add sugar to saucepan, bring to the boil, then pour over damsons. Allow to cool, then cover with a lid or cloth and leave overnight. The next day, strain off liquor into a saucepan, bring to the boil and pour over fruit, again leave overnight. Repeat once more. On the fourth day return fruit and liquor to pan and boil very gently for 15 to 20 minutes. Remove orange and spices, then pot fruit and syrup (see page 88), label and store in a cool, dark cupboard or the larder. Keep for 3 to 4 months. They will keep for about 3 weeks in the fridge once opened.

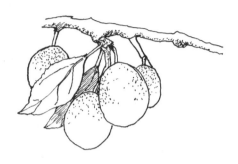

Damson Vinegar

This vinegar is wonderful when used to deglaze a pan in which you have been cooking pork.

2 lb (1 kg) damsons
32 fl oz (1 litre) wine vinegar

Place 1 lb (500 g) of the fruit in a saucepan, pour over vinegar and bring to the boil; boil for 1 minute. Pour into a large bowl, cover with a cloth and leave for 24 hours. Strain off most of the liquid into a saucepan and add remaining damsons. Bring to the boil, boil for 1 minute, then add to the bowl with the first damsons, cover again and leave a further 24 hours. Strain and bottle.

Damson Cheese

Fruit cheeses are thick and firm, they can be used to accompany game or cold meats instead of the more usual jellies but were often served as a dessert, so pour some of your cheese into shaped pots that can be turned out when you're ready to serve.

3 lb (1.5 kg) damsons
10 fl oz (315 ml) water
sugar, see method
almond oil, for coating

Simmer fruit with water in a preserving pan for 25 to 30 minutes until it is soft enough to push through a sieve. Measure sieved fruit and to every 20 fl oz (625 ml) allow 1 lb (500 g) sugar. Return fruit pulp to pan and reheat. Stir in sugar and cook gently until 'set' is reached (see page 88), stirring constantly. Brush storage jar or pots with almond oil and pour in cheese. Seal and store in the larder. This cheese improves with keeping for 3 to 4 months before eating.

The Maids keep their teeth very white, till they have lost the blue of their Plumb, and then they dye them as black as Jet.

(1727, A. Hamilton)

Damson Curd

This curd is strongly flavoured and delicious, use as a filling for cakes or tarts, or fold into whipped egg whites or cream to make a quick mousse.

1 lb (500 g) damsons
½ stick cinnamon
2 tablespoons water
8 oz (250 g) sugar
4 oz (125 g) butter
4 eggs, beaten well

In a saucepan with a tight-fitting lid simmer damsons and cinnamon in water until very soft, 20 to 25 minutes. Remove stones and sieve or purée in a blender or food processor. Put purée in the top of a double boiler and stir in sugar. Dissolve sugar over a gentle heat, then stir in butter cut into small pieces and when it is melted add beaten eggs and cook for 30 minutes over a gentle heat, stirring constantly, until mixture thickens. Pot (see page 88) and cover. Like most homemade curds this is best stored in the fridge, where it will keep for 2 to 3 months.

She was handsome in her time...
She has quite lost the blue on the Plum.
(1738, Jonathan Swift)

Greengage Conserve

A slightly more laborious way of making jam but worth it, for it does seem to conserve the greengage flavour rather more than the conventional modern methods do. This jam does not 'set' in the usual way, use it to fill cakes and tarts, or eat it with a spoon as the French do: it's delicious.

8 fl oz (250 ml) water
2 lb (1 kg) sugar
2 lb (1 kg) greengages

Place water and sugar together in a saucepan. Heat gently until sugar is dissolved, then boil fast for 5 minutes. Cool, then add the whole greengages, mix well, return pan to heat and boil until fruit is tender and begins to thicken a little – 15 to 20 minutes. The fruit will burst and the stones rise to the top, when they can be skimmed off with a slotted spoon. Pot (see page 88), store in a cool, dark place.

81

Damson Gin

Prick damsons all over and pack into clean jars. To every jar add 2 teaspoons sugar and 1 whole allspice. Pour over gin to fill the jar, seal tightly and store in a cool, dark place. Shake once or twice a week. Keep for 3 to 4 months before use. Serve diluted with tonic or lemonade as a refresher in summer, or with a dash of hot water to make a hot toddy in winter.

Wild fruits, particularly the plum, were gathered along streams and preserved in barrels of spring water over which a scum quickly formed. The plains dwellers were happy to have this sort of preserves even though it was sour and unpalatable. (Richard Osborn Cummings, The American and His Food)

Damson Syrup

Use this syrup diluted with water, soda water, lemonade or a sparkling mineral water to make a refreshing drink.

4 lb (2 kg) very ripe damsons
2 lb (1 kg) sugar
60 fl oz (1.9 litres) water
thinly pared peel and juice of 3 oranges
wine vinegar, see method

Pick over damsons carefully, removing any damaged fruit. Place in a large, shallow bowl and crush with a wooden spoon, pressing hard to extract juice and flavour. In a heavy saucepan, gently dissolve sugar in water, then boil hard for 5 minutes. Add orange peel to damsons and pour over orange juice. Mix well, crushing and pressing as you do so. Pour over boiling syrup, stir, cover with a cloth and leave for 24 hours. Strain off syrup, re-boil and pour over fruit. Leave for 48 hours, then strain through a fine sieve or jelly bag, re-boil and bottle. Cork and store in a cool place. A tablespoon of best quality wine vinegar may be added to each 20 fl oz (625 ml) of strained fruit juice at the re-boiling stage, if desired, for a sharper flavour.

He knew to tame to Plums the Sourness of the Sloes

BASICS

Plain Shortcrust Pastry
Suitable for savoury and sweet tarts.

8 oz (250 g) flour
1/2 teaspoon salt
4 oz (125 g) butter or margarine, hard and cold
3–4 tablespoons ice-cold water

Sift flour and salt into a mixing bowl. Cut fat into flour using two knives or a pastry cutter and mix briefly in a food processor or rub in with fingertips. When mixture looks like breadcrumbs, add water and draw together; the mixture should be very stiff. Knead together against the sides of the bowl, then wrap in plastic wrap and leave in a cool place or the bottom of the fridge for 30 minutes or until you wish to use it. If left for several hours or overnight, the pastry should be brought to room temperature for 2 to 3 hours before use.

Rough Puff Pastry

An alternative to puff pastry: use for sweet or savoury dishes.

8 oz (250 g) flour
1/2 teaspoon salt
4 oz (125 g) butter
2 oz (60 g) lard
4–6 tablespoons ice-cold water

Sift flour and salt into a mixing bowl. Cut fats into flour using a knife – the pieces need not be very small. Make a well in the mixture, add water and mix the dough to an elastic consistency.

Turn out onto a floured board and knead. Roll into a long strip, flour lightly, then fold in three and seal the edges with the rolling pin. Give the pastry a half turn, roll out again, flour again, fold and seal. Turn again and roll out a third time; the fat should now be evenly distributed, if not, roll out a fourth time. Fold again, wrap in plastic wrap and leave in a cool place or the fridge until needed.

Pancakes

Makes about eight 7 in (17.5 cm)
pancakes
4 oz (125 g) plain flour
1 whole egg
1 egg yolk
3 tablespoons brandy
7–8 fl oz (220–250 ml) skimmed milk
good quality cooking oil

Sieve flour into a bowl and make a well in the centre. Add egg, egg yolk, brandy and milk, and, using a wire whisk or electric beater, beat well until mixture is smooth and light. Leave to rest in a cold place for 30 minutes. The mixture can be left longer – any time up to 2 hours.

Pour 3 tablespoons cooking oil into a heated heavy-bottomed frying pan and swirl to coat, then pour off surplus oil and reserve for next pancake. Heat oil, then pour in enough batter to give a very thin layer covering the bottom of the pan. Cook for 1–1½ minutes over a medium-hot heat lifting edges with a palette knife to check that pancake is not burning – it should be cream and golden when it is cooked. When ready, turn with the help of palette knife and cook other side. Remove and place on a warm plate. Cover with slightly damp absorbent kitchen paper and keep warm in a very low oven until ready to use. Make each pancake the same way, pouring off oil in between.

To Test Jam for Set

Remove saucepan or preserving pan from heat and put a little jam or jelly on to a cold plate. Leave to cool, then tilt the plate slightly. The jam is setting if it begins to wrinkle at this point.

If using a sugar thermometer, 'set' is reached at 110°C/220°F.

To Pot Jam, Curd or Preserves

Potting must be done correctly to keep food from developing bacteria.

Make sure that the jars are completely sterile, warm and dry. Remove any foam that may have formed on the surface of the liquid and pot carefully and quickly. Fill jars to the brim, cover with wax circles, then seal with self-sealing lids. Label and store in a cool, dark place or the fridge, as directed.

Freezing

Plums are not ideal fruit for freezing but when you have an excess, it is a quick and simple way of preserving them for later use in pies, tarts, puddings and purées.

Use firm, ripe fruit and always remove the stones. Plums discolour in the freezer, so, if freezing raw, dip them in a solution of the juice of 1 lemon to 20 fl oz (625 ml) water, then pack and wrap in the normal way.

They can also be frozen raw with a cooked syrup poured over. Dip halved and stoned plums in the lemon and water solution as before, then pack tightly into plastic containers. Pour over a syrup of 8 oz (250 g) sugar dissolved in 20 fl oz (625 ml) water. Cool syrup before using. Alternatively freeze as a purée, see page 66.

Greengages are not good freezers; damsons on the other hand do keep their flavour. Treat as above but do not remove stones as the fruit is too small. Do not store for longer than 3 months.

A great platter of plum-porridge of pleasure wherein is stued the mutton of mistrust.
(1591, Lyly, Endymion)

INDEX

*All plums are under Venus and are like women –
some better and some worse.*

(Culpeper)